One

Can

NEVER

Predict

the

Past

One
Can
NEVER
Predict
the
Past

Poems by

Peter Waldor

Cover design by Shay Culligan
Cover image *A Mask Sounds the Funeral Knell,* plate three
(Odilon Redon French, 1840–1916)
via Art Institute of Chicago on Unsplash
Author photo by Gabriel Waldor

ISBN: 978-1-63980-994-3

Kelsay Books
502 South 1040 East, A-119
American Fork, Utah 84003
Kelsaybooks.com

for Nizhóní

Other Books by Peter Waldor

Door to a Noisy Room
The Wilderness Poetry of Wu Xing
Who Touches Everything
The Unattended Harp
State of the Union
Gate Posts with No Gate
Nice Dumpling
Owl Gulch Elegies
Unmade Friend
Something About the Way
The Way 2
Midwife vs Obstetrician
Hats Off
Seven Quilts (essays)
Snowy Saplings
Understandings and Misunderstandings
At the Next Table
Time Can't Tell It's Being Told
Beginning Polyamory
Fairy Slippers
wellwhadayasay?
Turnstiles
14 Meditation Prompts and a Treatise on Noble Silence
The Third Way
You Alone Know
Tapadawhirld
Immigration Is the Essence of Democracy
Intermediate Polyamory
The Way Fourth

Contents

There
is
nothing
more
sacrilegious
than
religion

If
no
king,
then
no
king
of
kings

Branches
below
Roots
above

Sketching
a
tree
is
the
artist's
great
test

Lend
Borrow
Giggle
Guffaw

Soar
Dive
Float
Sigh

Forget
to
ask
the
question
and
you
just
may
get
the
right
answer

Humidifiers
dehumidifiers
and
too
many
spare
rooms

There
is
nothing
worse
than
a
sore
winner

All
white
people
think
they
are
unusual
for
white
people

Don't
be
clever
when
being
clever

Smart
people
often
forget
the
names
of
their
bosses

The
best
words
are
those
used
for
lack
of
better
words

Brevity
is
the
mother
of
invention

Grand
finales
everywhere
always

Nocturnes
in
the
morning
and
aubades
at
night

When
civilization
ends
all
roads
will
become
beautiful

Never
take
any
vehicular
contrivance
any
further
than
you
can
walk
home
if
it
breaks

Discovery
is
nothing
other
than
rediscovery

The
haystack
has
always
been
in
the
needle

Writing
is
noticing
but
don’t
forget
the
small
matter
of
the
words

Be
the
devil
and
not
possessed
by
the
devil

Nothing
more
truthful
than
propaganda

Salespeople
are
the
worst
sellers

Wars
to
end
all
wars
never
end

May
everyone
be
a
limousine
liberal

The
poet
needs
the
poem
before
to
find
the
poem
after

The
pencil
is
mightier
than
the
pen

There
can
only
be
metaphorical
stillness

Yesterday
is
a
present
for
tomorrow

If
you
have
too
much
to
say
don’t
be
tempted
to
say
nothing
at
all

If
you’re
feeling
crabby
then
walk
like
a
crab
(sideways)
and
you
just
may
laugh

It
must
be
very
dark
to
grab
an
invisible
cup

The
grin
of
judgment
and
the
scowl
of
acceptance
are
one

If
you
don’t
say
hello
to
everyone
then
don’t
say
hello
to
anyone

In
flirting
the
desire
for
the
other
is
implausibly
deniable

Sing
for
yourself
while
you
are
singing
for
your
supper

No
one
will
ever
sing
the
song
they
came
to
sing

X

Good is good and evil is evil but to say

good and evil is problematic

Everyone hates the sound of their own voice

Orators must have extreme hatred

Some people look for trouble and don’t
find it and some find it without looking

Institutions designed to keep people out of trouble always
get them into more trouble, e.g. government, marriage, religion

Just because the world thinks you are invisible

doesn't mean you can't learn to be invisible

The jury is always out

and the court jester is always in

In your final instructions don't leave guidance
    as to who should give your eulogy

Never forget most good deeds go
    unpunished and a few are even praised

Best to live in places that had monarchies but don't anymore

rather than places that have one now or never had one

When a great teacher retires fly every

flag in the world at half-mast

Hell hath no fury greater than

a minnow struck by a pebble

A young man wants to show everyone his favorite music

An old man wants to hear about everyone else's favorite music

You are either a creature that stops

when it shits or one who keeps moving

Don't be a proximal pacifist, that is, one who is peaceful

in person but may endorse far away violence

Find a place with no cairns

so they need not be kicked down

Sad for a thing to be ruined,

but nothing worse than ruining the old ruin

Republicans tend to be the worst Republicans

Some Democrats aren't bad Democrats

If you are a magnet for fake intellectuals

then you are most likely a fake intellectual. Sorry

The praying mantis is usually an atheist

Corruption fighters are usually corrupt

Big government small government no government

Three bad answers to the essay question

When an infinity of doors close, one door cracks

open, surrounded by a rectangle of light

Terrible to get a disposable fork, knife

and spoon when just a fork will do

X

Way back the Buddha said *My kingdom for three pennies*
He was lucky, someone gave him three worn coins
That new king, the buyer, has slipped from every memory

All people are larger than life. All amoebas are larger
than life. All wrapping paper yearns
to be the parchment of the Dead Sea Scrolls

Brutus says *Romans, countrymen,* then Antony says
Friends, Romans, Countrymen. Whoever the writer was
must have known friendship triumphs, even in tragedy

Write only where you're not supposed to write and about
things you're not supposed to write about in words not fit
for writing, then you just might write something worth reading

A boy leaps into the air to
better inhale the blue smoke
of fireworks. He stays suspended

Past Present Future—three upside-down cups
A grifter’s two balls shift under them
Every fool watching knows which cup is empty

Chronicle the pieces of trees in your life, including yard sticks and toothpicks, scalloped shingles and dories, two by fours and parquet, sawdust and decorative tissue paper

Don’t end at the beginning
Don’t begin at the end
Don’t flinch in the middle

Raphael used Michelangelo’s face for Heraclitus
Walt Disney used Paul Muni for Mickey Mouse
Always use someone else for your subject

Dickinson in the morning
Notorious B.I.G. midday
Whitman at night

Fresh growing forest of hoarfrost around a catch basin
makes me ask what is what isn't alive, just what
the branching crystals ask seeing me

Giant spruce/fir forest, trees lacquered with snow
Then all at once the snow shakes off one tree
One curtain dropping in a sea of curtains

I don’t lock the door and someone enters and apologizes
but it is I who should have apologized for not locking the door
or, there should always be two apologies

Some people walk on subway grates and others
walk around them, like the ones, when the sea
parted, who chose to swim in either side of the great rift

Someday it will be good to be fat again, so if you're skinny now, enjoy it while you can, and if you're fat, be patient, your time will come

X

A mother tells her child slow down while eating and a child

tells their mother to stop giving advice. Both should listen

Not all old men think about getting out of chairs

and not all young men don’t think about it

You’re okay if you check a locked door up to three times but if you
    check a fourth they should lock you up and throw away the key

The body is so big sometimes you can find a
    part that has never been touched

Find the solution, then find the problem. Then trick yourself

into thinking the problem came first

Beware Buddhists, shrinks, and podiatrists

They tend to give advice

If asked for your religion, answer exactly—Yazidi, Animist, Poly-
theistic Atheist, Pharisee, Episcopalian, Cosa Nostra Buddhist

If you're a freedom fighter there is a forty-five percent
chance you are not really fighting for freedom

Anarchy possibly, hierarchy not for a second

Patriarchy gag yourself with a ball gag

Are you one of the lucky ones who know little

but are able to teach many things to people who know a lot?

May all pilots wear pink tutus

  and choose with or without epaulettes

Sometimes it feels good to walk faster than everyone else

  and sometimes it feels good to walk slower than everyone else

If you find yourself exaggerating the remoteness

    of the village then stop telling the story

You have only a few days, after your parents die elderly deaths,

    to believe you are not elderly yourself

If I had a great song for every great song I forgot

there would be no time for anything but great songs

Disturbing someone's loneliness is both most

important and to be most beware of

Knowing when to listen and when not to listen is like the
    hummingbird knowing every turn between Paducah and
        Guadalajara

Always be a tourist
    and never be a tourist

The indigity of forgetfulness is worse

than the indignity of memory

Never make mountains into molehills,

make mountains into mountain ranges

It is said variety is the spice of life but the hottest

spice of all is consistency

In dancing, the goal

is perfect stillness

We look to poets to help us understand love, death, joy, sadness

They look to us for the same understanding, so no one is happy

There is no such thing

as crossdressing

X

Listen
to
people
who
suggest
nice
places
to
see
sunsets

Learn
from
the
elk
how
easy
it
is
to
leave
an
ideal
place

Dust
never
settles

Beauty
only
comes
with
age

There
can
be
nothing
more
innocent
than
guilty
pleasure

Naughtiness
is
next
to
godliness

You
who
see
portals
here
and
there —
there
are
portals
everywhere

Immigration
is
the
essence
of
democracy

Everything
rises
and
falls
at
once

All
land
is
stolen,
but
who
stole
what
when
matters

A
word
to
the
wise
means
beware
words
of
the
wise

He
was
damned
when
he
didn't
so
we'll
never
know
if
he'd
be
damned
if
he
did

Aesthetics
must
fail
for
art
to
proceed

The
second
thought
is
not
always
better
than
the
first
thought

Public
architecture
inspires
private
architecture

Dwell
on
what
you
found,
not
what
you
lost,
even
if
you
haven't
found
a
thing

Be
a
vulture
not
a
hawk

The
puffball
must
be
crushed
to
properly
puff

I
am
not
therefore
I
think

Imitation
is
the
least
sincere
form
of
flattery

One
can
NEVER
predict
the
past

It
is
not
the
question
itself
but
the
attention
to
detail
in
the
question

Nature
is
the
best
nurturer

Great
thoughts
are
like
your
tattoo
that
only
others
can
see

There
is
always
a
tree
above
tree
line

We
know
it's
easy
to stop
but
we
forget
it's
also
easy
to
start

The
hardest
thing
to
say
is
nothing
at
all

All
music
was
made
for
the
moment
in
which
it
was
made

The
best
spots
are
never
taken

Are
you
avoiding
someone
because
you
are
avoiding
yourself

I
came
I
saw
I
flowered

No
two
people
are
alike
but
three
or
more
always
are

Love
train
stations
Hate airports

The
odd
man
is
not
always
out

Groucho
Marx
and
Karl
Marx
are
one

Don’t
wait
too
long
to
switch
to
legitimate
business
interests

The
believer
and
the
non-
believer
are
both
infidels

There
is
nothing
more
religious
than
sacrilege

About the Author

Peter Waldor is the author of twenty-nine books of poetry, including *Who Touches Everything,* which won the National Jewish Book Award for poetry. He is also the author of a book of essays, *Seven Quilts.* His book *Gate Posts With No Gate* is a poetry-art collaboration with a group of visual artists. He was the 2014–2015 Poet Laureate of San Miguel County, Colorado. His poetry has appeared widely in magazines, including *Ploughshares, American Poetry Review, The Colorado Review, Fungi Magazine,* and *Mothering Magazine.* He lives in Ophir, Colorado.

www.ingramcontent.com/pod-product-compliance
Lightning Source LLC
Chambersburg PA
CBHW031201160426
43193CB00008B/463
* 9 7 8 1 6 3 9 8 0 9 9 4 3 *